MY FIRST BOOK

SWEDEN

ALL ABOUT SWEDEN FOR KIDS

GL🌐BED
CHILDREN BOOKS

Interior and cover Design: Daniel Day

Editor: Margaret Bam

For My Sons, Daniel, David and Jude

Scandinavia, Sweden

Sweden

Sweden is a **country**.

A country is land that is controlled by a **single government**. Countries are also called **nations, states, or nation-states**.

Countries can be **different sizes**. Some countries are big and others are small.

Malmö, Sweden

Where Is Sweden?

Sweden is located in the continent of **Europe**.

A continent is **a massive area of land that is separated from others by water or other natural features**.

Sweden is situated in the northern part of Europe.

Panorama of Stockholm, Sweden

Capital

The capital of Sweden is Stockholm.

Stockholm is located in the **eastern part** of the country.

Stockholm is the largest city in Sweden.

Gothenburg, Sweden

Counties

Sweden is a country that is made up of 21 counties.

The counties of Sweden are as follows:

Stockholm, Västerbotten, Norrbotten, Uppsala, Södermanland, Östergötland, Jönköping, Kronoberg, Kalmar, Gotland, Blekinge, Skåne, Halland, Västra Götaland, Värmland, Örebro, Västmanland, Dalarna, Gävleborg, Västernorrland and Jämtland.

Young Swedish girl at Midsummer

Population

Sweden has population of around **10 million people** making it the 91st most populated country in the world and the 15th most populated country in Europe.

Gammelstad, Lulea, Sweden

Size

Sweden is **450,295 square kilometres** making it the fifth largest country in Europe by area.

Sweden is the 56th largest country in the world.

Languages

The official language of Sweden is Swedish. The Swedish language originated in Sweden and is now spoken by millions of people across the world.

Sámi and Finnish are also spoken in Sweden.

Here are a few Swedish phrases
- **Hur mår du** - How are you?
- **God Morgon!** - Good morning

Royal Palace in Sweden

Attractions

There are lots of interesting places to see in Sweden.

Some beautiful places to visit in Sweden are

- Vasa Museum
- Liseberg
- Skansen
- Øresund Bridge
- The Royal Palace
- Stockholm City Hall

Malmo, Sweden

History of Sweden

People have lived in Sweden for a very long time, in fact Sweden's prehistory begins around 12,000 BC in the Allerød oscillation.

Sweden and its people were first described by Publius Cornelius Tacitus in his written work Germania, in which he described them as a powerful tribe with ships that had a prow at each end.

Sweden joined the European Union on 1st January 1995.

Young girl at Midsummer festival, Sweden

Customs in Sweden

Sweden has many fascinating customs and traditions.

- **Swedish people are very hospitable. It is customary to take off your shoes before entering the home of a Swedish family and to arrive with a small present for the host to say thank you.**
- **Many Swedish people enjoy spending time in nature, choosing to spend their free time in the forest or by the sea.**

Music of Sweden

There are many different music genres in Sweden such as **Swedish folk music, Pop, Progg, Swedish death metal and Polska.**

Some notable Swedish musicians include
- **ABBA**
- **Avicii**
- **Zara Larsson**
- **Roxette**
- **Robyn**

Swedish meatballs

Food of Sweden

Sweden is known for having delicious, flavoursome and rich dishes.

Sweden does not have a national dish, however many people consider **meatballs and lingonberries** to be the unofficial national dish of the country. Meatballs and lingonberries is Swedish meatballs served with Lingonberry jam.

Food of Sweden

Some popular dishes in Sweden include

- **Kroppkakor**
- **Falukorv**
- **Filmjölk**
- **Toast Skagen**
- **Räkmacka**
- **Herring**
- **Husmanskost**

Uppsala, Sweden

Weather in Sweden

Most of Sweden has a temperate climate with largely four distinct seasons and mild temperatures throughout the year.

The warmest month is July.

Reindeers in Lapland, Sweden

Animals of Sweden

There are many wonderful animals in Sweden.

Here are some animals that live in Sweden

- Wolf
- Lynx
- Moose
- White Moose
- Arctic Fox
- Reindeer

Kebnekaise

Mountains

There are many beautiful mountains in Sweden which is one of the reasons why so many people visit this beautiful country every year.

Here are some of Sweden's mountains

- **Kebnekaise**
- **Sarektjåkkå**
- **Storvätteshågna**
- **Åreskutan**
- **Kaskasatjåkka**

Football with Sweden flag

Sports of Sweden

Sports play an integral part in Swedish culture. The most popular sport is **Football.**

Here are some of famous sportspeople from Sweden

- **Zlatan Ibrahimović - Football**
- **Ingemar Stenmark - Skiing**
- **Jan-Ove Waldner - Table tennis**
- **Johnny Oduya - Ice hockey**
- **Thomas Ravelli - Football**

Alfred Nobel (1833-1896)

Famous

Many successful people hail from Sweden.

Here are some notable Swedish figures

- **Alfred Nobel – Chemist**
- **Ingrid Bergman – Actress**
- **Greta Garbo – Actress**
- **Ingvar Kamprad – Businessman**
- **Alexander Skarsgård – Actor**

Gustav I Vasa King of Sweden (1496 – 1560)

Something Extra...

As a little something extra, we are going to share some lesser known facts about Sweden.

- Over half of Sweden is covered in forest.
- Sweden is home to an extraordinary Ice Hotel.
- The name for Sweden derives from the Proto-Indo-European root *s(w)e, meaning "one's own".
- Gustav I Vasa was the first truly autocratic Swedish sovereign and was a skilled propagandist.

Words From the Author

We hope that you enjoyed learning about the wonderful country of Sweden.

Sweden is a country rich in culture and beauty, with lots of wonderful places to visit and people to meet.

We hope you continue to learn more about this wonderful nation. If you enjoyed this book, consider leaving a review!

With Love

Made in United States
North Haven, CT
02 October 2023

42275291R00027